Jamba 1.5
The AI Hybrid Shaking Up Open-Source Models

A Deep Dive into AI21 Labs' Revolutionary Architecture and What It Means for the Future of Artificial Intelligence

Alejandro S. Diego

Copyright © Alejandro S. Diego, 2024.

All rights reserved. No part of this publication may be reproduced, distributed, or transmitted in any form or by any means, including photocopying, recording, or other electronic or mechanical methods, without the prior written permission of the publisher, except in the case of brief quotations embodied in critical reviews and certain other noncommercial uses permitted by copyright law.

Table of Contents

Introduction...3
Chapter 1: The Evolution of Language Models.........6
Chapter 2: The Birth of Jamba 1.5............................12
Chapter 3: Understanding the Hybrid Architecture 18
Chapter 4: The Mamba Component and Its Advantages...25
Chapter 5: Benchmark Performance and Testing...32
Chapter 6: Speed and Efficiency in Enterprise Applications..38
Chapter 7: Quantization and Resource Efficiency.. 45
    How Developers Benefit from Deploying Jamba 1.5 on Limited Hardware..50
Chapter 8: Multilingual Support and Global Applications...53
    Examples of Potential Use Cases in Diverse Linguistic Environments..58
Chapter 9: Developer-Friendly Features..................62
    ChatGPT said:... 62
Chapter 10: Open-Source Commitment and Accessibility..69
Conclusion..75

Introduction

AI21 Labs has established itself as a pioneering force in the artificial intelligence field, gaining widespread recognition for its contributions to language models and natural language processing (NLP). Their work with the Jurassic language models, in particular, has positioned them as innovators capable of pushing the boundaries of AI technology. These models have enabled developers and researchers to perform more complex tasks, and AI21 Labs' commitment to open-source solutions has earned them a solid reputation for fostering collaboration and accessibility within the AI community.

The introduction of the Jamba 1.5 models marks a significant advancement in the open-source AI landscape. These models, Jamba 1.5 Mini and Jamba 1.5 Large, have been designed with a hybrid architecture that blends cutting-edge techniques to boost AI performance. This hybrid approach combines the best features of Transformer models with Structured State Space Models (SSM), allowing them to handle larger context windows more efficiently than their predecessors. What makes Jamba 1.5 stand out is its ability to process long sequences of data without slowing down, making it ideal for tasks that require deep contextual understanding, such as complex generative AI reasoning or summarizing lengthy documents.

Open-source AI has become a cornerstone of innovation, allowing researchers, developers, and businesses to experiment freely and build upon each other's work. The availability of open-source models like Jamba 1.5 democratizes access to advanced AI, breaking down barriers and fostering a collaborative environment that accelerates the pace of technological progress. By making these powerful tools available to the broader community, AI21 Labs empowers a wide range of users to explore new possibilities in AI development, driving forward innovation across industries.

Chapter 1: The Evolution of Language Models

The development of language models has been a transformative journey in the field of artificial intelligence. Early attempts at creating AI that could understand and generate human language relied on rule-based systems, which, while groundbreaking at the time, were limited by their inability to handle the complexity and nuance of natural language. As technology advanced, researchers moved toward statistical models that could learn from vast amounts of text data. This shift laid the foundation for modern AI language models, culminating in the development of deep learning techniques and the introduction of the Transformer architecture.

The Transformer model, introduced by Vaswani et al. in 2017, marked a significant leap forward in natural language processing (NLP). It allowed AI systems to process language more effectively by enabling parallelization and focusing on context through attention mechanisms. Transformers quickly became the backbone of many state-of-the-art language models, including GPT, BERT, and others, powering applications ranging from chatbots to content generation tools.

AI21 Labs entered the scene with its groundbreaking contributions, most notably the Jurassic series of language models. These models were built on the foundation of Transformer architecture but were designed to handle even more complex tasks with greater efficiency. AI21 Labs focused on making these models highly versatile, enabling them to perform a wide range of language-related tasks, such as text generation, summarization, and translation.

Jurassic models demonstrated AI21 Labs' commitment to pushing the boundaries of what AI could achieve. By improving the scalability and efficiency of their models, they helped bridge the gap between cutting-edge research and practical, real-world applications. AI21 Labs' decision to make these models available on open platforms like Hugging Face further underscored their dedication to fostering a collaborative environment within the AI community.

With the introduction of the Jamba 1.5 models, AI21 Labs continued to build on its legacy of innovation. These new models reflect a deep understanding of the limitations of existing language models and present a hybrid solution that addresses some of the most significant challenges, such as handling long context windows. Their work not only advances the capabilities of AI but also contributes to the broader movement of making advanced technology accessible and useful to a wide range of users.

The rise of Transformer models transformed the landscape of natural language processing. The architecture, with its self-attention mechanism, allowed for more efficient and scalable processing of text compared to previous models. Transformers were able to capture context in ways that earlier models couldn't, leading to breakthroughs in various AI tasks like machine translation, text summarization, and question answering. Their strength lies in their ability to process input sequences in parallel, which not only speeds up computation but also enables them to focus on relevant parts of the text through the attention mechanism. This allows for much deeper context comprehension, resulting in more coherent and contextually accurate outputs.

Despite these strengths, Transformers are not without limitations. One of the most significant challenges faced by traditional Transformer models is their difficulty in handling large context windows. When tasked with processing long sequences of text, Transformers can become inefficient because they have to consider every part of the input equally, leading to substantial computational overhead. This results in slower processing times and higher memory usage, especially when the model is forced to work with extended sequences of data, such as entire books, long meeting transcripts, or comprehensive policy documents.

This limitation is particularly problematic for tasks that require the model to maintain an understanding of large amounts of contextual information over extended periods. As the context window increases, the model's ability to manage the data effectively decreases, causing it to either lose track of essential details or slow down considerably. This can result in hallucinations, where the model produces inaccurate or nonsensical outputs due to its inability to keep all the relevant information in memory.

AI21 Labs recognized this challenge and sought to address it with their Jamba 1.5 models. By introducing a hybrid architecture that combines the strengths of Transformers with more efficient methods like Structured State Space Models, they aimed to overcome the limitations of traditional models. This innovation allows the Jamba 1.5

models to process longer sequences without sacrificing speed or accuracy, making them far better suited for tasks that involve large context windows.

Chapter 2: The Birth of Jamba 1.5

The Jamba 1.5 models, introduced by AI21 Labs, represent a significant leap forward in the world of open-source AI. These models, available in two variants—Jamba 1.5 Mini and Jamba 1.5 Large—are designed to tackle some of the most persistent challenges in natural language processing. Unlike many traditional models that struggle with handling extended context windows, the Jamba 1.5 models feature a hybrid architecture that allows them to process much longer sequences of data efficiently. This makes them ideal for applications that require a deep understanding of context, such as summarizing long documents, analyzing lengthy conversations, or handling complex generative AI tasks.

The Jamba 1.5 Mini model is designed with developers and researchers in mind who need powerful capabilities but may not have access to massive computational resources. Despite its smaller size, Jamba 1.5 Mini packs impressive power, making it a practical option for a wide range of applications, from prototyping to deploying in production environments. Its ability to handle longer context windows, coupled with its resource efficiency, makes it a strong contender in the open-source space.

Jamba 1.5 Large, on the other hand, is built for those who need even greater performance. With a more extensive architecture, this model is optimized for tasks that require intensive computation and large-scale data processing. Jamba 1.5 Large shines in environments where accuracy, speed, and the ability to maintain complex context are crucial. Whether it's powering advanced chatbots, summarizing lengthy documents, or conducting complex reasoning, this model delivers exceptional results.

Both models share a common goal: to push the boundaries of what language models can achieve while remaining accessible to the open-source community. By offering these models through platforms like Hugging Face and cloud services like Google Cloud and Microsoft Azure, AI21 Labs ensures that developers, businesses, and researchers have the tools they need to explore and innovate with the latest in AI technology.

The hybrid architecture of Jamba 1.5 represents a significant innovation by blending the strengths of traditional Transformer models with the advantages of Structured State Space Models (SSM). This fusion addresses some of the key limitations that have plagued previous models, particularly when it comes to handling large context windows efficiently. By combining these two powerful approaches, Jamba 1.5 can manage longer sequences of data without the slowdown and inefficiency that typically burden Transformers in such scenarios.

The Transformer architecture is well-known for its ability to process text sequences in parallel, using self-attention mechanisms to capture context across a wide range of inputs. This has made it the go-to choice for many language models, but as the length of the input sequences increases, the model's efficiency diminishes. Transformers struggle with large amounts of data because they must attend to every part of the sequence at once, which can lead to increased computational costs and slower performance.

The Structured State Space Model (SSM) component of Jamba 1.5 addresses this challenge by introducing more efficient methods for managing sequences of data. SSMs leverage older, but still highly effective, neural network techniques, including elements from convolutional neural networks (CNNs). These methods are better suited for handling the kinds of computations needed for processing long sequences of information. Essentially, the SSM acts as a mechanism for maintaining and updating a smaller, more manageable state that captures the relevant context, allowing the model to process longer inputs more effectively.

By incorporating SSM into the hybrid architecture, Jamba 1.5 can strike a balance between the comprehensive attention mechanisms of Transformers and the efficiency of SSMs. This combination allows the model to retain the ability to capture detailed contextual information while minimizing the resource and time costs associated with processing large volumes of text. The result is a model that can tackle more complex tasks, such as summarizing lengthy documents or generating coherent responses in extended conversations, without sacrificing performance or accuracy.

This enhancement in performance and efficiency is crucial for real-world applications where handling large context windows is often necessary. Whether it's summarizing legal documents, analyzing long meeting transcripts, or powering AI systems that need to remember previous interactions, the hybrid architecture of Jamba 1.5 ensures that the model can perform these tasks with greater speed and precision.

Chapter 3: Understanding the Hybrid Architecture

The SSM Transformer within Jamba 1.5 is a core component that enables the model to excel at handling long sequences of data. To understand its role, it's essential to break down both the Transformer and Structured State Space Model (SSM) components and how they work together to create a more efficient and powerful system.

Traditional Transformers rely on self-attention mechanisms that allow the model to focus on different parts of the input text simultaneously. This is incredibly effective for tasks that involve shorter sequences or require capturing relationships between words or phrases spread across the text. However, the Transformer architecture's major limitation is its inefficiency when processing long sequences, as it must compute attention across every part of the input. This leads to increased memory usage and slower processing times, especially when the text is extensive.

The SSM Transformer addresses this issue by integrating Structured State Space Models into the architecture. SSMs, unlike Transformers, don't require full attention to every part of the sequence at once. Instead, they rely on structured neural networks that use state-based approaches to process sequences more efficiently. This allows the model to manage and update a smaller, compressed state that retains the essential contextual information without needing to hold all the details in memory at once.

In simple terms, the SSM Transformer is like having a specialized memory that only keeps track of the most relevant information, allowing the model to focus on what matters while ignoring unnecessary details. This makes it far more efficient when dealing with longer sequences of data.

One of the primary benefits of this approach is that it reduces the computational load significantly. While a traditional Transformer needs to expend a lot of resources to handle large context windows, the SSM component streamlines the process by only focusing on the key parts of the data. This efficiency is particularly beneficial in tasks where the model needs to process extended sequences, such as generating responses to long conversations, analyzing lengthy documents, or performing tasks that require deep contextual understanding.

The hybrid architecture that combines the Transformer and SSM components enables Jamba 1.5 to manage large context windows without the slowdown typically associated with processing such volumes of data. This allows the model to maintain its performance even as the complexity of the task increases, making it ideal for applications that require handling extensive context efficiently. In Jamba 1.5, the SSM Transformer serves as a critical innovation that bridges the gap between the flexibility of Transformers and the efficiency of more structured neural network models.

The hybrid model of Jamba 1.5 efficiently processes longer sequences of data by leveraging the complementary strengths of both the Transformer architecture and Structured State Space Models (SSM). Traditional Transformers are known for their ability to capture complex relationships in text by processing sequences in parallel, which works well for shorter inputs. However, when the data becomes extensive, Transformers struggle because they must compute attention across the entire input, leading to inefficiency. This is where the hybrid approach comes into play.

By combining Transformers with SSM, the Jamba 1.5 models can effectively manage large sequences without suffering from the performance issues typical of traditional models. The SSM component introduces a state-based processing mechanism that allows the model to retain and update relevant contextual information while reducing the computational burden. This results in a more efficient handling of long data sequences, where only the most crucial information is kept in memory, and the model doesn't need to reprocess everything continuously. This reduces the amount of time and resources required to complete tasks, making the model faster and less resource-intensive, even when working with extensive datasets.

The benefits of this architecture extend to real-world applications where handling large volumes of data is essential. For businesses, this hybrid model can significantly improve the efficiency of various operations that rely on natural language processing. For instance, in customer service, a chatbot powered by Jamba 1.5 can remember and process longer conversations without slowing down, providing more accurate and contextually relevant responses to users. In the legal or financial sectors, where long documents like contracts or reports need to be analyzed, Jamba

1.5 can summarize and extract key information much faster than traditional models, saving time and reducing the likelihood of errors.

In more complex applications, such as business intelligence or document management, the ability to efficiently process long sequences of data is crucial. Businesses often deal with large datasets, including meeting transcripts, policy documents, and research papers. Jamba 1.5's architecture allows for faster and more accurate processing of these materials, enabling decision-makers to access the insights they need without delays. This can also be a game-changer in fields like healthcare, where analyzing extensive patient records or research data quickly and accurately is critical for making informed decisions.

Overall, the hybrid architecture of Jamba 1.5 provides a practical solution to the limitations of traditional models, making it a powerful tool for businesses and industries that require the processing of long sequences of data efficiently. Its ability to maintain speed, accuracy, and resource efficiency in real-world applications makes it a standout option in the AI landscape.

Chapter 4: The Mamba Component and Its Advantages

The Mamba component of the Jamba 1.5 models is a critical part of their architecture, developed with insights from researchers at Carnegie Mellon and Princeton. Mamba addresses one of the most significant challenges faced by traditional Transformer models: efficiently handling longer context windows without compromising on performance. By incorporating the latest advancements in AI research, Mamba helps the Jamba 1.5 models achieve superior speed, resource efficiency, and contextual comprehension.

At its core, Mamba is designed to optimize the attention mechanism of the model. Traditional Transformers rely on a full self-attention mechanism that requires processing all parts of the input sequence equally, which can be computationally expensive and slow, particularly when dealing with extensive text. Mamba, however, introduces a more efficient approach to attention by keeping a smaller, continually updated state as it processes the data. This allows the model to maintain focus on the most relevant parts of the sequence, reducing the need for the entire context to be considered at every step.

This smaller state not only makes the model faster but also significantly reduces its memory footprint. Traditional Transformers require large amounts of memory to process long sequences, which can strain computational resources. Mamba's efficient attention mechanism alleviates this burden by streamlining the process, allowing the model to handle longer sequences with far less memory. This makes the Jamba 1.5 models much more practical for deployment in environments where hardware resources may be limited or where scaling is a priority.

The insights from Carnegie Mellon and Princeton researchers that shaped Mamba's development revolve around the concept of making attention mechanisms more efficient without sacrificing the depth of understanding required for complex tasks. By focusing on optimizing how the model manages context, Mamba enhances the model's ability to work with extended data sequences in a way that traditional approaches cannot match.

In practice, this means that Jamba 1.5, equipped with the Mamba component, is capable of performing complex tasks like multi-hop reasoning, document retrieval, and large-scale question answering with greater efficiency. The model can keep relevant information in memory longer, ensuring more accurate outputs while reducing the need for repetitive processing of the same data. This translates into real-world benefits such as faster response times and lower costs in high-demand applications, whether in customer service, content generation, or enterprise data management.

The Mamba component exemplifies the impact of cutting-edge AI research on improving model performance. By addressing the specific challenges of attention mechanisms and memory efficiency, it allows Jamba 1.5 to perform tasks that require deep contextual understanding more effectively than traditional models, all while being more resource-conscious.

Mamba's efficient attention mechanism is designed to handle longer context windows by streamlining how the model processes information. Traditional Transformers use full self-attention, which requires the model to calculate attention across every part of the input sequence. This approach works well for short sequences but becomes increasingly inefficient as the context window grows. The larger the input, the more computation is needed, leading to slower performance and higher memory usage. This becomes a significant bottleneck when dealing with tasks that involve long documents, conversations, or extensive datasets.

Mamba tackles this problem by introducing a more targeted approach to attention. Instead of processing the entire sequence equally, Mamba maintains a smaller state that gets continuously updated as the model processes the data. This smaller state focuses on retaining only the most relevant information, allowing the model to prioritize what is important while discarding less critical details. By doing this, Mamba reduces the computational load and speeds up the processing time, even for long sequences.

This efficient attention mechanism means that Mamba doesn't need to attend to every part of the input all at once. Instead, it updates its understanding of the context as it processes new information, which significantly cuts down on memory usage. In contrast, traditional Transformers need to keep track of all the information in the sequence simultaneously, leading to greater resource consumption. Mamba's ability to focus on what matters allows the Jamba 1.5 models to perform better with less strain on hardware, making them more practical for real-world applications where resource efficiency is critical.

When comparing Mamba to traditional Transformer models, the differences in speed and resource efficiency become clear. Transformers are powerful but can become sluggish and resource-intensive when dealing with longer sequences. This is because every time a new piece of information is added to the sequence, the model has to reprocess the entire context, which can slow down operations significantly. Mamba, on the other hand, avoids this by updating its state dynamically, which allows the model to process information incrementally and more efficiently.

This dynamic updating mechanism makes Mamba much faster when handling tasks that require an understanding of extended context. For example, when summarizing a long document or conducting complex generative reasoning, Mamba can produce results quicker than a traditional Transformer because it doesn't have to repeatedly process the entire input. This efficiency translates directly to real-world benefits, such as lower operational costs, faster response times, and the ability to run the model on less powerful hardware.

In essence, Mamba's efficient attention mechanism provides a solution to one of the most pressing limitations of Transformer models: the difficulty in managing long context windows. By focusing on updating relevant information incrementally rather than processing everything at once, Mamba enables the Jamba 1.5 models to achieve better performance while using fewer resources, making them faster and more practical for a variety of applications.

Chapter 5: Benchmark Performance and Testing

AI21 Labs developed the custom benchmarking tool called Ruler to evaluate and measure the performance of their Jamba 1.5 models across a variety of tasks. Ruler was designed to test how effectively these models handle complex language processing challenges, particularly those that require managing long context windows and performing intricate reasoning tasks.

What sets Ruler apart from other benchmarking tools is its focus on evaluating real-world applications and the specific strengths of the hybrid architecture in Jamba 1.5. Traditional benchmarks often measure models based on more general metrics, such as accuracy in language generation or translation tasks. However, Ruler is tailored to assess how well a model performs in tasks that demand the processing of extensive sequences of data, which is one of the defining features of Jamba 1.5.

Ruler includes tests for tasks like multi-hop tracing, where the model must follow and process information across multiple steps, and retrieval and aggregation, where the model needs to extract relevant data from long texts and compile it accurately. These are tasks that would typically challenge models that struggle with context retention, but Jamba 1.5's hybrid architecture, powered by Mamba and SSM, was designed to excel in these areas.

The benchmarking tool also evaluates question answering, particularly in scenarios where the questions require understanding large amounts of context or dealing with complex relationships between pieces of information. By pushing the models through these demanding tests, Ruler helps AI21 Labs ensure that Jamba 1.5 can deliver consistent performance in real-world situations where processing long context windows is essential.

Ruler's creation underscores AI21 Labs' commitment to not only developing advanced models but also rigorously testing them against the kinds of challenges that users will encounter in practical applications. By providing a detailed, task-specific benchmark, AI21 Labs can confidently demonstrate the advantages of Jamba 1.5 over traditional models, particularly in areas where handling large context windows and complex data relationships are critical.

The performance of Jamba 1.5 models stands out when compared to competitors like LLaMA 3.17b and MiSTra Large 2, particularly in tasks that demand handling extensive context windows and complex reasoning. The custom benchmarking tool, Ruler, revealed that Jamba 1.5 consistently outperformed these models in key areas such as multi-hop tracing, retrieval, aggregation, and question answering. These tasks, which require the model to manage and process long sequences of data efficiently, are areas where traditional models often struggle.

One of the main reasons Jamba 1.5 outshines its competitors is its hybrid architecture. While models like LLaMA and MiSTra rely heavily on traditional Transformer mechanisms, which can become inefficient with large context windows, Jamba 1.5 incorporates Structured State Space Models (SSM) alongside its Transformer architecture. This combination allows Jamba 1.5 to maintain relevant context more effectively while using fewer resources. As a result, it delivers faster, more accurate outputs in tasks that require deep contextual understanding.

In benchmark tests, Jamba 1.5 Mini and Jamba 1.5 Large outperformed models like LLaMA 3.17b and MiSTra Large 2 across several demanding scenarios. For example, Jamba 1.5 Large achieved a remarkable score of 65.4 on the Ruler benchmarks, significantly surpassing its competitors. This superior performance demonstrates the model's ability to handle complex, real-world challenges, which is a crucial advantage for developers and enterprises looking to implement advanced AI solutions.

The real-world implications of these benchmarks are significant for developers and businesses alike. For developers, Jamba 1.5's enhanced performance means they can build more sophisticated applications that rely on handling large amounts of context without sacrificing speed or accuracy. This can include everything from customer support chatbots that need to manage long conversations to AI tools that must summarize or analyze extensive documents.

For enterprises, these benchmarks translate into practical benefits like increased efficiency, lower costs, and improved outcomes. In industries where processing large datasets is common—such as legal, financial, or healthcare sectors—using a model like Jamba 1.5 can lead to faster decision-making and more accurate results. The reduced computational demands also make it easier to deploy these models in resource-constrained environments, broadening their accessibility and impact.

Ultimately, the performance comparisons show that Jamba 1.5 models are not only faster and more efficient than their competitors but also more capable of tackling the complex, context-heavy tasks that are becoming increasingly vital in real-world applications. This makes them an appealing choice for both developers looking to push the boundaries of AI and enterprises seeking to implement cutting-edge solutions.

Chapter 6: Speed and Efficiency in Enterprise Applications

Speed is a critical factor in enterprise AI use cases, directly impacting efficiency, user experience, and overall operational success. In business environments where AI is deployed, the ability to process information quickly and deliver timely results can be the difference between gaining a competitive edge or falling behind. Whether it's in customer service, data analysis, or decision-making tools, the speed of an AI model can make or break its value to an organization.

In customer-facing applications like chatbots or virtual assistants, speed is essential for delivering seamless user experiences. Customers expect quick, accurate responses, and delays can lead to frustration, diminished trust, and even lost business. AI models like Jamba 1.5, which excel in processing long conversations efficiently, can respond in real-time, making interactions smoother and more satisfying for users.

In operational contexts, speed becomes even more critical when dealing with large volumes of data. Enterprises often need to process vast datasets—whether it's analyzing customer feedback, summarizing legal documents, or generating business intelligence reports. A slower AI model can create bottlenecks, delaying decisions and hampering productivity. Models like Jamba 1.5, with their ability to handle extensive context without slowing down, ensure that businesses can operate at the pace required by modern demands.

Furthermore, speed in AI models translates into cost savings. Faster models reduce the need for extensive computational resources, allowing businesses to run their operations more efficiently. This is particularly important in large-scale deployments where the cost of running AI models can be substantial. With models like Jamba 1.5, which are designed to perform faster while using less memory, enterprises can achieve the desired results without incurring unnecessary expenses.

In industries where time-sensitive decisions are crucial—such as finance, healthcare, or logistics—speed is not just a luxury but a necessity. AI models that can deliver rapid, accurate insights enable businesses to act quickly, whether it's identifying market trends, diagnosing a patient's condition, or optimizing supply chain operations. The speed advantage of models like Jamba 1.5 empowers enterprises to stay agile and responsive in fast-paced environments, making them better equipped to meet their goals and serve their customers effectively.

Ultimately, speed in AI models impacts every facet of enterprise operations, from improving customer satisfaction to enhancing decision-making and reducing costs. The ability of models like Jamba 1.5 to deliver faster results with high accuracy makes them an invaluable asset for businesses looking to leverage AI technology in a meaningful and impactful way.

Jamba 1.5 models achieve up to 2.5 times faster performance through their innovative hybrid architecture, which combines the best elements of Transformers and Structured State Space Models (SSM). This approach allows them to handle long sequences of data more efficiently by reducing the computational overhead associated with traditional attention mechanisms. Unlike traditional Transformer models that require attention to be distributed across every part of the input sequence, Jamba 1.5 utilizes a more focused and dynamic state-based system through the Mamba component. This system continuously updates relevant information without needing to reprocess the entire context, leading to faster computations and quicker responses.

Another factor contributing to Jamba 1.5's speed advantage is its optimized attention mechanism. The Mamba component uses a smaller memory state that is easier to manage, which allows the model to process longer context windows without slowing down. By streamlining this process, Jamba 1.5 minimizes the need for excessive computational resources, which directly impacts the model's performance. This means that the model can complete tasks faster and more efficiently, even when dealing with complex or large datasets.

In addition to speed, Jamba 1.5 models are designed with a lower memory footprint and improved hardware efficiency. Traditional models often require significant computational power and memory, which can be a limiting factor for businesses that don't have access to high-end infrastructure. Jamba 1.5 addresses this challenge by optimizing its memory usage, allowing it to run effectively on less powerful hardware.

This lower memory footprint is particularly beneficial for businesses that need to deploy AI at scale but want to keep infrastructure costs manageable. By reducing the demand for expensive, high-performance hardware, Jamba 1.5 models enable businesses to implement AI solutions more cost-effectively. This is especially advantageous for startups, small businesses, or any organization looking to maximize the return on their AI investments without needing to upgrade their hardware.

For enterprises, the combination of faster performance and hardware efficiency means greater productivity and lower operational costs. Whether it's deploying AI for customer service, content generation, or data analysis, businesses can benefit from quicker results without the need to invest in extensive computational resources. This also makes Jamba 1.5 more accessible for a broader range of applications, from small-scale deployments to large, enterprise-level AI initiatives.

In summary, Jamba 1.5 models achieve their speed and efficiency through a combination of innovative architecture and memory optimization. This not only results in faster performance but also reduces the hardware demands, making AI more practical and cost-effective for businesses across different industries.

Chapter 7: Quantization and Resource Efficiency

The Experts INT8 quantization technique is an advanced method that AI21 Labs developed to optimize the performance and efficiency of their Jamba 1.5 models. Quantization, in general, is a process used in machine learning to reduce the precision of the numbers that represent a model's parameters, which can significantly decrease memory usage and computational demands without a noticeable drop in model performance. Experts INT8 is a specific approach to quantization that targets the weights within the mixture of experts (MoE) layers of the model.

In deep learning models, particularly large ones like Jamba 1.5, the weights (which represent the learned parameters of the model) can take up a significant amount of memory. Typically, these weights are stored with high precision, usually in a 32-bit floating-point format. While this level of precision is necessary for training, it is often excessive for inference, where the model makes predictions. Quantization reduces the precision of these weights, typically down to an 8-bit integer format, hence the name INT8. This reduction in precision drastically lowers the memory requirements and speeds up computation.

The "Experts" part of the technique refers to how AI21 Labs applied this quantization specifically to the mixture of experts (MoE) layers of the model. These layers are responsible for much of the model's complexity and account for a large portion of the model's weights—often up to 85%. By quantizing these layers, AI21 Labs managed to significantly reduce the overall size of the model without sacrificing too much in terms of accuracy or performance. This makes the model not only faster but also more resource-efficient.

One of the key innovations in the Experts INT8 technique is that AI21 Labs designed it to dynamically dequantize the weights during runtime, directly within the GPU. This means that while the model's weights are stored in a more compact 8-bit format, they are converted back to a higher precision just as they are needed for computation. This dynamic dequantization ensures that the model retains a high level of performance while benefiting from the efficiency gains of quantization.

The result is that Jamba 1.5 models can fit more comfortably on hardware with limited resources, such as a single 8-GPU node, while still maintaining their full functionality. For developers and businesses, this means that deploying these models in real-world applications is more feasible, even in environments where computational resources are at a premium.

The Experts INT8 quantization technique is a sophisticated method that reduces the memory and computational demands of the Jamba 1.5 models by compressing their weights without compromising their performance. This makes the models faster, more efficient, and more accessible for deployment in a variety of hardware environments, which is a significant advantage for developers and enterprises looking to implement AI solutions at scale.

The Experts INT8 quantization technique optimizes memory and computational costs by reducing the precision of the model's weights, specifically targeting the mixture of experts (MoE) layers, which are responsible for a significant portion of the model's parameters. By converting these weights from their typical 32-bit floating-point format to an 8-bit integer format, the technique dramatically decreases the model's memory requirements and speeds up computation. This reduction in precision might sound like it could affect the model's performance, but the clever implementation of dynamic dequantization ensures that quality remains high.

Dynamic dequantization occurs directly on the GPU during runtime, meaning that even though the model's weights are stored in a more compact format, they are converted back to higher precision just when needed for calculations. This real-time adjustment allows the model to retain much of the accuracy and performance of a full-precision model, even though it's operating with far less memory. The key is in balancing precision and efficiency, ensuring that the model performs complex tasks effectively without consuming unnecessary resources.

The result is that Jamba 1.5 models, despite being highly complex and capable of processing long sequences of data, can run on hardware that is less powerful than what would typically be required. This optimization leads to lower computational costs, as the need for high-end, expensive infrastructure is reduced. Businesses and developers can deploy these models more cost-effectively, making AI solutions more accessible across different industries.

How Developers Benefit from Deploying Jamba 1.5 on Limited Hardware

Case Study 1: Startups and Small Businesses
Startups and smaller businesses often face budget constraints when it comes to deploying AI models. High-performance GPUs and extensive cloud resources can be expensive, making it challenging to implement advanced AI solutions. By using the Experts INT8 quantization technique, developers working in these environments can deploy Jamba 1.5 models on more affordable hardware setups without compromising on performance. For example, a customer service startup could implement an AI-driven chatbot that handles complex, long conversations on a limited number of GPUs, reducing infrastructure costs while maintaining high-quality interactions with customers.

Case Study 2: Research and Education
Academic institutions and research labs often operate with limited hardware resources compared

to commercial enterprises. Deploying large AI models can be a challenge when resources are shared among many researchers or when budgets are tight. With Jamba 1.5's optimized memory usage, researchers can run sophisticated models on smaller setups. This opens up opportunities for advanced AI research in institutions that might not have access to the latest hardware, enabling breakthroughs in areas like natural language processing or AI ethics research, without needing to compromise on the scale or complexity of the models being used.

Case Study 3: Large-Scale Enterprises with Distributed Systems Even large enterprises can benefit from Jamba 1.5's ability to run efficiently on limited hardware, particularly in distributed systems where AI models are deployed across multiple locations or devices. For instance, a multinational corporation running AI models in customer service centers around the world could deploy Jamba 1.5 on a distributed network of less powerful machines, saving costs on infrastructure while still delivering fast, high-quality AI services. The lower memory footprint and computational demands also reduce energy consumption, aligning with sustainability goals that are increasingly important to large corporations.

In each of these cases, the Experts INT8 quantization technique allows developers and businesses to harness the power of Jamba 1.5 models on limited hardware, without sacrificing quality. This flexibility makes it easier for a wide range of users to implement advanced AI solutions, even when working within resource constraints.

Chapter 8: Multilingual Support and Global Applications

Jamba 1.5's support for multiple languages is a key feature that enhances its versatility and broadens its potential applications across various industries and regions. By offering capabilities in languages such as English, Spanish, French, Portuguese, Italian, Dutch, German, Arabic, and Hebrew, Jamba 1.5 is designed to cater to a global audience, enabling businesses and developers to implement AI solutions that meet the needs of diverse linguistic communities.

This multilingual support is crucial for several reasons. In a world where businesses operate across borders, the ability to communicate in multiple languages is essential for effective customer service, localized content creation, and global market expansion. Jamba 1.5's capability to understand

and generate text in these languages allows companies to automate and streamline processes in multiple regions without needing separate AI models for each language.

For example, a company operating in both Europe and Latin America can use Jamba 1.5 to power customer service chatbots that handle inquiries in English, Spanish, French, Portuguese, and German. This reduces the need for creating and maintaining different models for each language, simplifying deployment and management while ensuring consistent quality across all interactions. The model's ability to switch between languages also allows for smoother operations in multicultural environments, where users may communicate in more than one language.

From a technical perspective, Jamba 1.5's multilingual support means that developers can build applications that reach a broader audience without needing to worry about language limitations. Whether it's generating localized content, translating documents, or understanding and processing inputs in different languages, Jamba 1.5 provides the flexibility needed to meet these challenges. This is particularly valuable in industries like e-commerce, customer service, education, and media, where language diversity is a daily reality.

In addition, the model's support for languages beyond English addresses a growing demand for AI tools that cater to non-English-speaking populations. While many AI models have historically focused on English, the expansion to other major languages makes Jamba 1.5 more inclusive and applicable in regions where English is not the primary language. This aligns with the global trend toward greater inclusivity in technology, ensuring that AI advancements benefit a wider spectrum of users.

By supporting multiple languages, Jamba 1.5 opens up opportunities for businesses and developers to engage with diverse markets more effectively, providing a robust tool for multilingual communication, content creation, and customer service. This capability not only enhances the model's usability but also ensures that AI solutions can be tailored to meet the specific needs of various linguistic and cultural contexts.

The multilingual capabilities of Jamba 1.5 are particularly significant in global business settings, where companies often need to operate in multiple languages to engage with diverse customers, employees, and partners. In today's interconnected world, businesses are not confined by geographical boundaries, and their success often depends on their ability to communicate effectively across different regions and cultures. AI models that can support multiple languages offer a strategic advantage by enabling seamless operations across borders, improving customer service, and enhancing localization efforts.

Multilingual AI capabilities allow businesses to create consistent and efficient processes in various linguistic environments. For example, a global company might have offices in Europe, Asia, and Latin America, each region requiring different languages for customer interactions, internal communications, and marketing efforts. With Jamba 1.5, businesses can automate these interactions without needing separate models for each language, reducing complexity and ensuring uniformity in the quality of the AI's outputs across all languages.

This multilingual functionality is particularly valuable for customer service operations, where companies need to provide support in the native language of their customers. Whether through chatbots, virtual assistants, or automated email responses, Jamba 1.5 enables businesses to respond to customer inquiries in their preferred language, which enhances the customer experience and fosters loyalty. The ability to communicate effectively in a customer's native language can make a significant difference in how the brand is perceived, leading to higher satisfaction and better retention rates.

Examples of Potential Use Cases in Diverse Linguistic Environments

1. Multinational E-commerce Platforms: E-commerce businesses operating globally need to cater to customers in various regions, each with its own language preferences. Jamba 1.5 can be used to generate product descriptions, respond to customer inquiries, and create marketing content in multiple languages. This allows the platform to localize its offerings more effectively, making it easier for customers to navigate, understand, and engage with the brand. The model's multilingual support ensures that customers feel understood and valued, regardless of their language.

2. Global Customer Service Centers: Companies that manage customer service centers across different countries can benefit from Jamba 1.5's ability to support multiple languages in a single model. Instead of training separate models for each language, a unified system powered by Jamba 1.5 can handle customer inquiries in English, Spanish, French, and other languages, all from the same AI platform. This reduces operational complexity, lowers costs, and allows for more efficient management of global customer service operations.

3. International Media and Content Creation: Media companies that produce content for a global audience often need to generate articles, social media posts, or videos in multiple languages. Jamba 1.5 can assist in creating localized content that resonates with specific audiences, allowing for better engagement across different markets. Whether it's generating news articles in French, social media posts in Spanish, or marketing materials in Portuguese, the model's multilingual support ensures that content can be tailored to suit each region's linguistic and cultural preferences.

4. Cross-border Healthcare Services: Healthcare providers that operate in multilingual regions or serve international patients can use Jamba 1.5 to streamline communication. For instance, AI-powered chatbots can provide medical information or appointment scheduling in the patient's preferred language, while the model's ability to process medical records or research papers in multiple languages can enhance collaboration among international healthcare professionals. This capability is particularly important in regions with diverse linguistic populations, where providing care in the patient's native language can improve understanding and outcomes.

5. Global Education Platforms: Online education platforms that offer courses to students from around the world can leverage Jamba 1.5 to provide learning materials, quizzes, and feedback in different languages. This allows the platform to cater to students in their preferred language, making education more accessible and personalized. Instructors can also use the model to translate course content or communicate with students from different linguistic backgrounds more effectively, enhancing the overall learning experience.

In summary, the significance of multilingual capabilities in global business settings cannot be overstated. Whether it's improving customer service, localizing content, or enhancing communication in multinational organizations, Jamba 1.5's ability to operate across languages opens up a wide range of possibilities for businesses operating in diverse linguistic environments. These capabilities not only help companies reach broader audiences but also ensure that they can engage with customers, employees, and partners in a way that feels personal and effective, no matter where they are located.

Chapter 9: Developer-Friendly Features

citation generation

ChatGPT said:

ChatGPT

Jamba 1.5 models come equipped with built-in support for structured JSON output, function calling, and citation generation, making them highly versatile tools for developers and businesses alike. These features not only enhance the model's functionality but also open up new possibilities for building sophisticated AI applications.

The ability to generate structured JSON output is particularly valuable in scenarios where the model needs to provide data in a format that can be easily processed by other systems. JSON (JavaScript Object Notation) is a widely used data format, particularly in web development and APIs, because of its simplicity and readability. When Jamba 1.5 outputs data in a structured JSON format, it allows for seamless integration with various applications, whether it's feeding information into a database, powering a web interface, or facilitating communication between different parts of a software system. This built-in support means that developers can rely on the model to generate outputs that are immediately usable without the need for extensive post-processing.

Function calling is another powerful feature that makes Jamba 1.5 models stand out. In many AI-driven applications, the ability to interact with external tools or systems is crucial. Jamba 1.5's function-calling capability allows it to trigger specific actions or retrieve information from external systems based on the model's outputs. For example, a virtual assistant powered by Jamba 1.5 could be configured to make API calls, schedule tasks, or perform actions within other software environments automatically, based on user inputs or internal triggers. This makes the model far more than just a passive generator of text; it becomes an active participant in executing workflows and tasks within a broader system.

Citation generation is another valuable feature, particularly in contexts where the credibility and traceability of information are essential. When using Jamba 1.5 for tasks like research assistance, content creation, or report generation, the model can provide citations that refer back to its sources of information. This capability is critical in fields such as journalism, academia, and professional writing, where ensuring the accuracy and traceability of claims is a top priority. By incorporating citations into its outputs, Jamba 1.5 helps users maintain the integrity of their work while also reducing the manual effort involved in tracking down sources.

Together, these features—structured JSON output, function calling, and citation generation—make Jamba 1.5 models highly adaptable to a wide range of real-world applications. Whether developers are building AI-powered tools for automation, integrating the model into existing software systems, or using it to generate content that requires verifiable sources, Jamba 1.5 provides the functionality needed to support complex, multifaceted workflows.

Jamba 1.5 models come equipped with built-in support for structured JSON output, function calling, and citation generation, making them highly versatile tools for developers and businesses alike. These features not only enhance the model's functionality but also open up new possibilities for building sophisticated AI applications.

The ability to generate structured JSON output is particularly valuable in scenarios where the model needs to provide data in a format that can be easily processed by other systems. JSON (JavaScript Object Notation) is a widely used data format, particularly in web development and APIs, because of its simplicity and readability. When Jamba 1.5

outputs data in a structured JSON format, it allows for seamless integration with various applications, whether it's feeding information into a database, powering a web interface, or facilitating communication between different parts of a software system. This built-in support means that developers can rely on the model to generate outputs that are immediately usable without the need for extensive post-processing.

Function calling is another powerful feature that makes Jamba 1.5 models stand out. In many AI-driven applications, the ability to interact with external tools or systems is crucial. Jamba 1.5's function-calling capability allows it to trigger specific actions or retrieve information from external systems based on the model's outputs. For example, a virtual assistant powered by Jamba 1.5 could be configured to make API calls, schedule tasks, or perform actions within other software environments automatically, based on user inputs or internal triggers. This makes the model far more than just a passive generator of text; it becomes an active participant in executing workflows and tasks within a broader system.

Citation generation is another valuable feature, particularly in contexts where the credibility and traceability of information are essential. When using Jamba 1.5 for tasks like research assistance, content creation, or report generation, the model can provide citations that refer back to its sources of information. This capability is critical in fields such as journalism, academia, and professional writing, where ensuring the accuracy and traceability of claims is a top priority. By incorporating citations into its outputs, Jamba 1.5 helps users maintain the integrity of their work while also reducing the manual effort involved in tracking down sources.

Together, these features—structured JSON output, function calling, and citation generation—make Jamba 1.5 models highly adaptable to a wide range of real-world applications. Whether developers are building AI-powered tools for automation, integrating the model into existing software systems, or using it to generate content that requires verifiable sources, Jamba 1.5 provides the functionality needed to support complex, multifaceted workflows.

Chapter 10: Open-Source Commitment and Accessibility

AI21 Labs has shown a strong commitment to the open-source community by making Jamba 1.5 models freely available under an open model license. This decision reflects their belief in democratizing access to advanced AI technologies and fostering collaboration within the global AI community. By releasing Jamba 1.5 as open-source, AI21 Labs invites developers, researchers, and businesses to experiment with and build upon these models, promoting innovation without the barriers typically associated with proprietary software.

Keeping Jamba 1.5 open-source is significant for several reasons. First, it empowers a broader audience to leverage cutting-edge AI capabilities without the financial and technical restrictions that often accompany closed-source models. Open-source models can be used, modified, and adapted to specific needs, making them accessible to startups, small businesses, and academic researchers who might not have the resources to invest in expensive AI infrastructure. This accessibility drives innovation across a wider spectrum of industries and applications.

Additionally, AI21 Labs' commitment to open-source aligns with the broader trend of collaborative development in the AI space. When models like Jamba 1.5 are open for the community to access, it enables collective problem-solving and shared progress. Developers can contribute improvements, find new use cases, and explore unique implementations, which in turn accelerates the evolution of AI technology as a whole. This collaborative approach ensures that the technology does not remain in the hands of a few but instead benefits a diverse global community.

The availability of Jamba 1.5 on multiple platforms and cloud services—such as Hugging Face, Google Cloud, Microsoft Azure, and Nvidia NIM—further underscores AI21 Labs' dedication to making these models as accessible and easy to use as possible. By providing a range of deployment options, AI21 Labs ensures that developers can choose the platform that best fits their needs, whether they're working on a small project or a large-scale enterprise deployment.

In short, AI21 Labs' commitment to keeping Jamba 1.5 open-source is a bold move that supports the growth and accessibility of AI technology across the globe. By making these powerful models freely available, they are not only promoting innovation but also contributing to a more inclusive and collaborative AI ecosystem.

The Jamba Open Model License, which governs the use of Jamba 1.5, is designed to provide developers and researchers with the freedom to explore, experiment, and build upon the model while also ensuring responsible usage. This license grants users the ability to access, modify, and deploy Jamba 1.5 in their own projects, whether they are personal experiments, academic research, or commercial applications. However, like most open model licenses, it likely comes with certain conditions that aim to balance openness with ethical considerations, such as preventing misuse or harmful deployments.

For developers, the Jamba Open Model License means access to cutting-edge AI technology without the restrictive costs or limitations of proprietary models. They can integrate Jamba 1.5 into their projects, customize it for specific needs, and contribute back to the community, all while retaining flexibility over how they use the model. For researchers, the license enables them to study the model in detail, run experiments, and publish findings that could contribute to the broader understanding of AI technology.

One of the key benefits of the open model license is that it encourages innovation through collaboration. Developers can share their improvements or adaptations of the model with the community, helping to drive the evolution of AI technology as new ideas and approaches are tested and implemented. This also makes the technology more transparent, as the model's architecture, performance, and limitations can be openly studied and discussed.

In addition to its licensing flexibility, Jamba 1.5 is available on a range of platforms and cloud services, making it easy to deploy in different environments. Developers and businesses can choose the platform that best suits their needs, from smaller-scale projects to enterprise-level applications.

One key platform where Jamba 1.5 can be accessed is Google Cloud's Vertex AI, which allows developers to integrate the model into Google's scalable cloud infrastructure, leveraging its capabilities for AI-driven applications at scale. Microsoft Azure is another option, providing seamless integration with Microsoft's suite of cloud tools, enabling businesses to deploy AI models in an enterprise environment that requires security, compliance, and scalability. Nvidia's NIM platform also supports Jamba 1.5, allowing developers to take advantage of Nvidia's powerful GPU acceleration for faster AI processing.

Beyond these platforms, AI21 Labs is also working on expanding availability to other cloud providers, such as Amazon's Bedrock and the Databricks Marketplace, further enhancing the flexibility and accessibility of Jamba 1.5. This wide range of deployment options ensures that developers and businesses can implement the model in a variety of settings, depending on their specific infrastructure and requirements.

In essence, the Jamba Open Model License and the wide availability of Jamba 1.5 across multiple platforms make it a versatile and accessible tool for developers and researchers alike. Whether you're working on a small experiment or a large-scale commercial application, the combination of flexible licensing and diverse deployment options allows for seamless integration into virtually any project.

Conclusion

The ability to handle extensive context windows is becoming increasingly important in the world of artificial intelligence. As businesses and developers tackle more complex and data-intensive tasks, AI models need to manage larger amounts of information while maintaining speed and accuracy. Traditional models have often struggled with these demands, leading to inefficiencies and limitations in real-world applications. Jamba 1.5, with its hybrid architecture, introduces a solution that sets a new standard for handling these challenges.

Jamba 1.5 achieves a remarkable balance between speed, efficiency, and versatility. By combining the strengths of Transformer models with Structured State Space Models (SSM) and incorporating innovations like the Mamba component and Experts INT8 quantization, it can process long sequences of data without the slowdown typically associated with traditional models. This hybrid approach not only optimizes performance but also reduces the resource demands, allowing the model to run efficiently on a wide range of hardware. The model's ability to generate structured outputs, perform function calling, and even provide citation generation further expands its usability across diverse applications.

Jamba 1.5 sets a new benchmark in the AI landscape, particularly for industries that require the processing of large context windows, such as finance, legal, healthcare, and customer service. Its built-in multilingual support, combined with its fast performance, makes it a powerful tool for global enterprises seeking to automate and enhance their operations across multiple regions and languages. Developers, startups, and established companies alike can benefit from the flexibility and accessibility that Jamba 1.5 offers, thanks to its open-source nature and wide availability across leading cloud platforms.

Looking ahead, the impact of Jamba 1.5 on the future of AI development is poised to be substantial. By addressing some of the most pressing limitations of previous models, it opens up new possibilities for building more advanced AI applications. As the demand for AI continues to grow in various industries, Jamba 1.5 stands out as a model that can meet these evolving needs efficiently and effectively. Its contribution to AI development will likely inspire further innovations and set the stage for the next generation of AI models that prioritize both performance and accessibility.

In conclusion, Jamba 1.5 represents a significant step forward in AI technology, offering a versatile and powerful solution for developers and businesses alike. Its ability to handle extensive context windows, coupled with its efficiency and speed, positions it as a leading model in the AI space. As AI continues to transform industries and drive innovation, Jamba 1.5's hybrid architecture and open-source availability ensure that it will play a pivotal role in shaping the future of AI development and enterprise applications.

www.ingramcontent.com/pod-product-compliance
Lightning Source LLC
Chambersburg PA
CBHW070358230526
45471CB00006B/2630